Major European Union Nations

Major European Union Nations

Austria
Belgium
Czech Republic
Denmark
France
Germany
Greece
Ireland

Italy
The Netherlands
Poland
Portugal
Spain
Sweden
United Kingdom

Major European Union Nations

SPAIN

by
Rae Simons and Shaina C. Indovino

Mason Crest

Mason Crest
370 Reed Road, Broomall,
Pennsylvania 19008
www.masoncrest.com

Printed in the Hashemite Kingdom of Jordan.

First printing
9 8 7 6 5 4 3 2 1

Library of Congress Cataloging-in-Publication Data

Simons, Rae, 1957-
   Spain / by Rae Simons and Shaina C. Indovino.
      p. cm. — (The European Union : political, social, and economic cooperation)
   Includes index.
   ISBN 978-1-4222-2259-1 (hardcover) — ISBN 978-1-4222-2231-7 (series hardcover) — ISBN 978-1-4222-9274-7 (ebook)
   1. Spain—Juvenile literature. 2. European Union—Spain—Juvenile literature. I. Indovino, Shaina Carmel. II. Title.
   DP17.S487 2011
   946—dc22
                                                2010051847

Produced by Harding House Publishing Services, Inc.
www.hardinghousepages.com
Interior layout by Micaela Sanna.
Cover design by Torque Advertising + Design.

CONTENTS

SPAIN
European Union Member since 1986

Introduction

Sixty years ago, Europe lay scarred from the battles of the Second World War. During the next several years, a plan began to take shape that would unite the countries of the European continent so that future wars would be inconceivable. On May 9, 1950, French Foreign Minister Robert Schuman issued a declaration calling on France, Germany, and other European countries to pool together their coal and steel production as "the first concrete foundation of a European federation." "Europe Day" is celebrated each year on May 9 to commemorate the beginning of the European Union (EU).

The EU consists of twenty-seven countries, spanning the continent from Ireland in the west to the border of Russia in the east. Eight of the ten most recently admitted EU member states are former communist regimes that were behind the Iron Curtain for most of the latter half of the twentieth century.

Any European country with a democratic government, a functioning market economy, respect for fundamental rights, and a government capable of implementing EU laws and policies may apply for membership. Bulgaria and Romania joined the EU in 2007. Croatia, Serbia, Turkey, Iceland, Montenegro, and Macedonia have also embarked on the road to EU membership.

While the EU began as an idea to ensure peace in Europe through interconnected economies, it has evolved into so much more today:

- Citizens can travel freely throughout most of the EU without carrying a passport and without stopping for border checks.

- EU citizens can live, work, study, and retire in another EU country if they wish.

- The euro, the single currency accepted throughout seventeen of the EU countries (with more to come), is one of the EU's most tangible achievements, facilitating commerce and making possible a single financial market that benefits both individuals and businesses.

- The EU ensures cooperation in the fight against cross-border crime and terrorism.

- The EU is spearheading world efforts to preserve the environment.

- As the world's largest trading bloc, the EU uses its influence to promote fair rules for world trade, ensuring that globalization also benefits the poorest countries.

- The EU is already the world's largest donor of humanitarian aid and development assistance, providing around 60 percent of global official development assistance to developing countries in 2011.

The EU is not a nation intended to replace existing nations. The EU is unique—its member countries have established common institutions to which they delegate some of their sovereignty so that decisions on matters of joint interest can be made democratically at the European level.

Europe is a continent with many different traditions and languages, but with shared values such as democracy, freedom, and social justice, cherished values well known to North Americans. Indeed, the EU motto is "United in Diversity."

Enjoy your reading. Take advantage of this chance to learn more about Europe and the EU!

Ambassador John Bruton,
Former EU President and Prime Minister of Ireland

Valencia, Spain

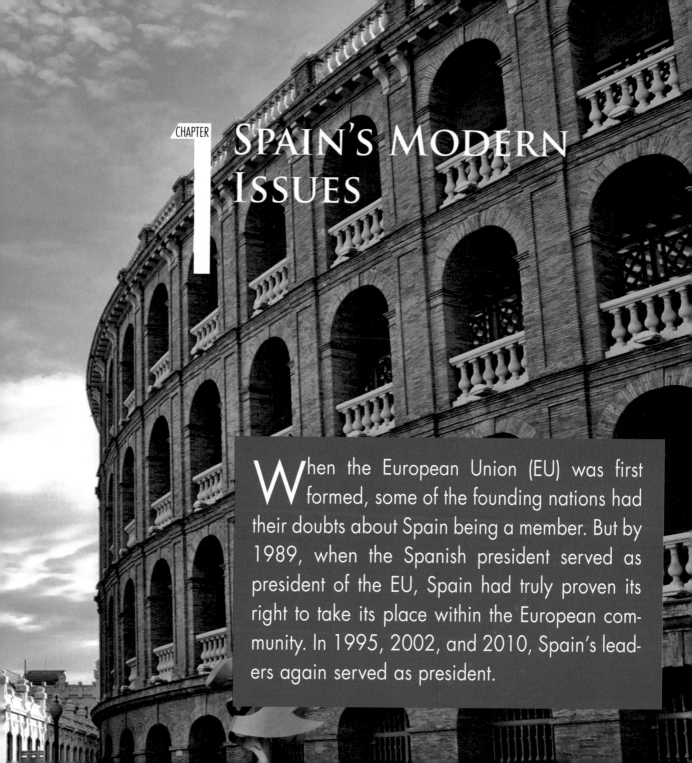

CHAPTER 1 SPAIN'S MODERN ISSUES

When the European Union (EU) was first formed, some of the founding nations had their doubts about Spain being a member. But by 1989, when the Spanish president served as president of the EU, Spain had truly proven its right to take its place within the European community. In 1995, 2002, and 2010, Spain's leaders again served as president.

The Formation of the European Union

The EU is a confederation of European nations that continues to grow. All countries that enter the EU agree to follow common laws about foreign security policies. They also agree to cooperate on legal matters that go on within the EU. The European Council meets to discuss all international matters and make decisions about them. Each country's own concerns and interests are important, though. And apart from legal and financial issues, the EU tries to uphold values such as peace and solidarity, human dignity, freedom, and equality. All member countries remain autonomous. This means that they generally keep their own laws and regulations. The EU becomes involved only if there is an international issue or if a member country has violated the principles of the union.

The idea for a union among European nations was first mentioned after World War II. The war had devastated much of Europe, both physically and financially. In 1950, French foreign minister Robert Schuman suggested that France and West Germany combine their coal and steel industries under one authority. Both countries would have control over the industries. This would help them become more financially stable. It would also make war between the countries much more difficult. The idea was interesting to other European countries as well. In 1951, France, West Germany, Belgium, Luxembourg, the Netherlands, and Italy signed the Treaty of Paris, creating the European Coal and Steel Community. These six countries would become the core of the EU.

In 1957, these same countries signed the Treaties of Rome, creating the European Economic Community. This combined their economies into a single European economy. In 1965, the Merger Treaty brought together a number of these treaty organizations. The organizations were joined under a common banner, known as the European Community. Finally, in 1992, the Maastricht Treaty was signed. This treaty defined the European Union. It gave a framework for expanding the EU's political role, particularly in the area of foreign and security policy. It would also replace national currencies with the euro. The next year, the treaty went into effect. At that time, the member countries included the original six plus another six who had joined during the 1970s and '80s.

In the following years, the EU would take more steps to form a single market for its members. This would make joining the union even more of an advantage. Three more countries joined during the 1990s. Another twelve joined in the first decade of the twenty-first century. As of 2012, six countries were waiting to join the EU.

The European Union works to unite European countries under one power.

WHO ARE THE BASQUE?

The original name for the Basques (and the one that Basques still use for themselves) is "Euskera." They are a very ancient and unique people who live in northern Spain and southwestern France. Their language is not related to any other language ever seen or recorded, and archeologists believe they have lived in the same region of Europe for thousands of years.

The ETA (Euskadi Ta Azkatasuna—meaning "Basque Homeland and Freedom") began in the 1960s as a student resistance movement against Franco, who was then the dictator of Spain. Under Franco, the Basque language was banned, their culture was suppressed, and many Basques were imprisoned and tortured for their political and cultural beliefs.

The Basques fought hard for freedom from Franco. When he died in 1975, the Basque region gained many rights. The Basques now have their own parliament and police force. Their government controls the education of their children, and it collects its own taxes. But the ETA and its supporters remained determined that the Basques needed full independence and freedom from the rest of Spain. After years of fighting without success, the ETA announced a ceasefire in 2010, followed by an end to armed conflict in 2011.

TERRORISM

THE ETA

In the twenty-first century, countries around the world are being forced to confront the issue of **terrorism**. When we think of terrorism, many times we connect the word to Islamic **extremists** from the Arab world—but Spain has had to deal with an altogether different terrorist group: the Basque Fatherland and Liberty (also known as the ETA).

The Basque region is in northern Spain, and a **radical** group there, wants to form its own nation, independent from the rest of Spain. This **separatist** group—the ETA—has carried out terrorist attacks ever since the early 1960s, causing nearly 850 deaths in all.

In March 2006, the ETA declared a ceasefire, saying it wished to use a peaceful **democratic** process to gain independence for the Basque region. Spaniards' reaction was divided: some people felt the Basques should have the right to form their own country, while others believed the Basques needed to accept their place as part of the entire nation. The Spanish government began working toward a lasting peace with the ETA, but this came to a halt when the ETA carried out a deadly bomb attack at Madrid's international airport.

Each time the ETA carried out a terrorist attack, anti-ETA demonstrations took place around the country, proving that most Spaniards, including the majority of Spain's Basque people, had no tolerance for ETA violence. In 2008, Spain signed an agreement with France that allowed Spanish law enforcement agents to operate in southwestern France against the ETA. Many of the ETA's leaders were arrested, and the group appeared to no longer be as strong.

Then, in September 2010, the ETA again announced a ceasefire. This time, the Spanish government did not trust the ETA's announcement, however. The government said it could not **negotiate** with the ETA unless the group would guarantee that it had given up violence for good. In 2011, ETA leaders confirmed that the ceasefire was permanent—but the Spanish government continues to watch the group carefully.

Radical Islam

Like much of the rest of the world, Spain has also had to deal with Islamic terrorists. The Spanish government is working hard to arrest and prosecute radical Islamic groups operating in Spain, and it is actively cooperating with other countries around the world, including the United States, to diminish the threat of terrorism.

In March 2004, ten bombs were set off on crowded trains during rush hour, killing 191 people. Evidence indicated that a radical Islamic group was responsible for the bombing. In 2007, Spain brought twenty-nine people to trial for their alleged role in the attack in Madrid. Twenty-one of the **defendants** were found guilty, although many of these were later **acquitted**. Three of the suspects were found guilty of murder and received sentences of over 42,000 years in prison.

Discrimination and Prejudice

Muslims have lived in Spain for hundreds of years; in fact, Muslims ruled a large part of Spain for about 800 years, until 1492. For the most part, Muslims and Christians have lived together peacefully, but the rise of extremist Islamic groups has caused **prejudice** against Muslims to flare up in Spain. Meanwhile, some Muslims in Granada and other parts of Spain are asking that they be allowed to have Muslim courts of law and special Muslim schools for their children. They also want an equal share in the money made from ticket sales at the Alhambra palace, which they regard as part of the cultural heritage of their Muslim ancestors.

Spain's increasingly negative feelings against Islam showed up in the Spanish **parliament** in a 2011 debate over whether to prohibit from all public spaces the body-covering burqa and the face-covering niqab worn by many Muslim women. The Spanish Senate eventually voted 131 to 129 to "use all options under our legal system and to proceed with rules to prohibit the public use of the burqa and the niqab to ensure equality, freedom, and security."

At the same time, the Muslim population in Spain is continuing to grow, mostly because of immigration from Muslim countries. The country now has a Muslim population of slightly more than a million (about 2 percent of Spain's total population), which means that today ten times as many Muslims live in Spain as were living there just twenty years ago. A Pew survey found that most Spaniards view Muslim immigrants with suspicion.

Muslims living in the EU face racism and discrimination because of their religion.

They doubt that Muslim immigrants will adopt the "Spanish way of life," and about 65 percent of Spaniards are worried about the growing presence of Islam in their nation.

Conservative Muslim beliefs about women conflict with the values of many Spaniards. In 2010, an imam (a Muslim religious leader) was arrested in Spain for forcing a Muslim woman to wear a head covering. In another case, conservative Muslims tried a woman for adultery and condemned her to death. (The woman escaped and fled to a police station before she could be executed.)

In response to incidents like these, many Spanish towns have passed their own laws against burqas. In some towns, women found wearing

Interior of a mosque in Andalusia, Spain.

Muslims in the European Union

Muslims are people who follow Islam, a religion that grew from some of the same roots as Judaism and Christianity. "Islam" means "submission to God," and Muslims try to let God shape all aspects of their lives. They refer to God as Allah; their holy scriptures are called the Qur'an, and they consider the Prophet Muhammad to be their greatest teacher.

About 16 million Muslims live in the European Union—but their stories vary from country to country. Some Muslim populations have been living in Europe for hundreds of years. Others came in the middle of the twentieth century. Still others are recent refugees from the troubled Middle East. By 2020, the Muslim population in Europe is predicted to double. By 2050, one in five Europeans are likely to be Muslim, and by 2100, Muslims may make up one-quarter of Europe's people.

Not all Europeans are happy about these predictions. Negative stereotypes about Muslims are common in many EU countries. Some Europeans think all Muslims are terrorists. But stereotypes are dangerous!

When you believe a stereotype, you think that people in a certain group all act a certain way. "All jocks are dumb" is a stereotype. "All women are emotional" is another stereotype, and another is, "All little boys are rough and noisy." Stereotypes aren't true! And when we use stereotypes to think about others, we often fall into prejudice—thinking that some groups of people aren't as good as others.

Fundamentalist Muslims want to get back to the fundamentals—the basics—of Islam. However, their definition of what's "fundamental" is not always the same as other Muslims'. Generally speaking, they are afraid that the influence of Western morals and values will be bad for Muslims. They believe that the laws of Islam's holy books should be followed literally. Many times, they are willing to kill for their beliefs—and they are often willing to die for them as well. Men and women who are passionate about these beliefs have taken part in violent attacks against Europe and the United States. They believe that terrorism will make the world take notice of them, that it will help them fight back against the West's power.

But most Muslims are not terrorists. In fact, most Muslims are law-abiding and hardworking citizens of the countries where they live. Some Muslims, however, believe that women should have few of the rights that women expect in most countries of the EU. This difference creates tension, since the EU guarantees women the same rights as men.

But not all Muslims are so conservative and strict. Many of them believe in the same "golden rule" preached by all major religions: "Treat everyone the way you want to be treated."

But despite this, hate crimes against Muslims are increasing across the EU. These crimes range from death threats and murder to more minor assaults, such as spitting and name-calling. Racism against Muslims is a major problem in many parts of the EU. The people of the European Union must come to terms with the fact that Muslims are a part of them now. Terrorism is the enemy to be fought—not Muslims.

burqas can be fined 600 euros ($750). A Muslim lawyer was thrown out of Spain's high court in Madrid because she wouldn't remove her hijab (headscarf), and a teenager in a Madrid high school was expelled for refusing to take off her headscarf.

Spain's position on this issue puts it in conflict with the European Union. The European Convention on Human Rights has warned Spain (and other nations that have passed similar laws against conservative Muslim dress) that these actions are an "ill-advised invasion of individual privacy." **Human rights activists** express their concern that the Spanish laws indicate **discrimination** against Muslims rather than true concern for women's rights.

SOCIALISM AND THE ECONOMY

Another issue that Spain faces in the twenty-first century is the conflict between its **socialist** policies and the demands of an ailing economy. Since

It is illegal for Muslim women in Spain to wear their traditional coverings in public.

Most young people in Spain are either unemployed or in jobs which don't pay enough for them to live on.

it became a democracy after the fall of Franco, Spain has been a socialist nation that provides welfare benefits for its citizens—but when Spain plunged into an **economic recession** in 2009, the government cut back many of these benefits.

In May 2011, throngs of Spanish young people staged peaceful demonstrations in 150 cities across Spain, protesting unemployment, social welfare cutbacks, and government **corruption**. Although unemployment is a big problem for everyone in Spain (the overall jobless rate is 22.8 percent, the highest in the **industrialized** world), it's even worse for Spain's young workers: nearly half of Spain's youth are unemployed, and the other half often face unfair working conditions. Many college graduates are forced to work in poorly paid **apprenticeships**, where they may only earn 640 euros ($900) a month, for ten years or more. Since this is not enough money to live on, these young people often end up living with their parents until they are in their mid-thirties. According to a recent survey, more than half of Spanish youth say they have no purpose in life and nearly all of them believe they are worse off than their parents.

These are all serious issues that Spain faces. And yet Spain also has many strengths on which to build, and its membership in the European Union means that it can depend on the EU's help.

One of Spain's greatest strengths is its long and proud history, combined with the rich cultural traditions of its people.

Fuengirola Castle in Málaga Province is a reminder of Spain's ancient history.

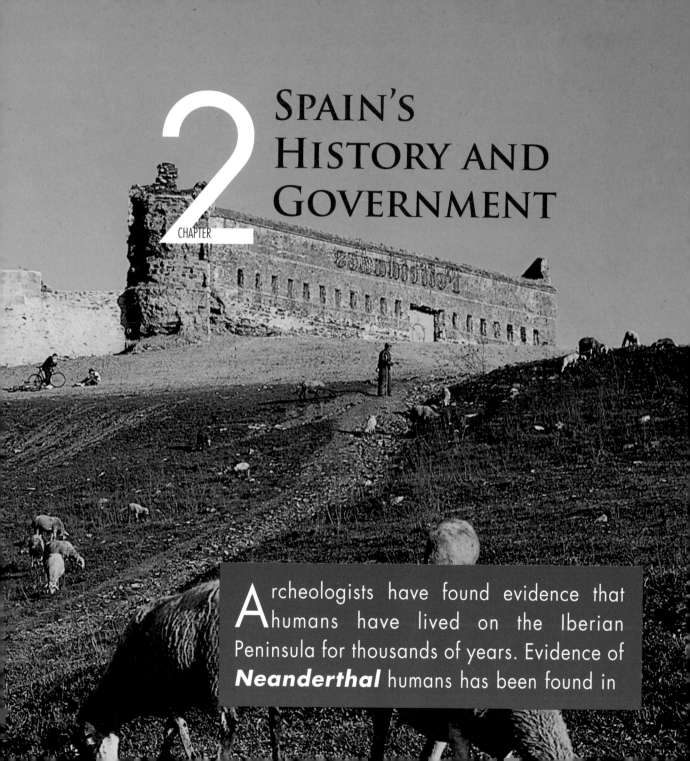

2 CHAPTER

SPAIN'S HISTORY AND GOVERNMENT

Archeologists have found evidence that humans have lived on the Iberian Peninsula for thousands of years. Evidence of **Neanderthal** humans has been found in

Gibraltar dating back 50,000 years, and modern humans arrived on the scene somewhere between 8000 and 4000 BCE, when the Iberians moved into Spain from the east. The Phoenicians sailed in from the east, creating trading posts along Andalusia's seaboard. Later, around 800 BCE, the Celts (the same people who settled Ireland and Scotland) arrived in the northern third of the peninsula. By 500 BCE, the Carthaginians from Northern Africa had colonized what is now southern Spain.

SPAIN AND THE ROMAN EMPIRE

In 206 BCE, the Roman Empire invaded Spain. The Roman soldiers easily crushed the native resistance and soon transformed the Iberian Peninsula into one of Rome's richest and most organized colonies. The Romans built paved roads that crisscrossed the peninsula, and they sailed their **galleys** up the Guadalquivir, all the way to Córdoba, where they loaded olive oil and wine into their holds for exportation to Rome.

When the Roman Empire adopted Christianity in the fourth century CE, Spain also became a Christian land. The Roman influence was strong on Spanish culture, and today's modern Spanish language still holds strong echoes of Rome's Latin.

THE VISIGOTHS AND THE MOORS

When the Roman Empire collapsed in the fifth century, waves of **barbarian** tribes swept across Europe. The Visigoths, a warlike Germanic people who migrated from central Europe, eventually took control of Spain.

Their rule was chaotic and disorganized, however, and eventually, in 711, the Moors swept in from Northern Africa. These Muslim people ruled the Iberian Peninsula for more than seven centuries. As Europe's Christian nations grew in power, however, they gradually drove the Moors further and further south. The last Moorish kingdom, Granada (the eastern half of modern-day Andalusia), fell in 1492 to the Catholic monarchs Isabella and Ferdinand. The Moors' cultural legacy can still be seen in Spain, especially in monuments such as the Mosque of Córdoba and the Alhambra Palace in Granada.

SPAIN AND THE NEW WORLD

Spain played an important role in the discovery of new land on the other side of the Atlantic, since King Ferdinand and Queen Isabella were the sponsors of Christopher Columbus's voyage of exploration. Columbus was followed by the **conquistadors**, who brought great wealth from the New World to Spain. As the conquistadors conquered more and more of the Americas' Native people, Spain built a vast overseas empire.

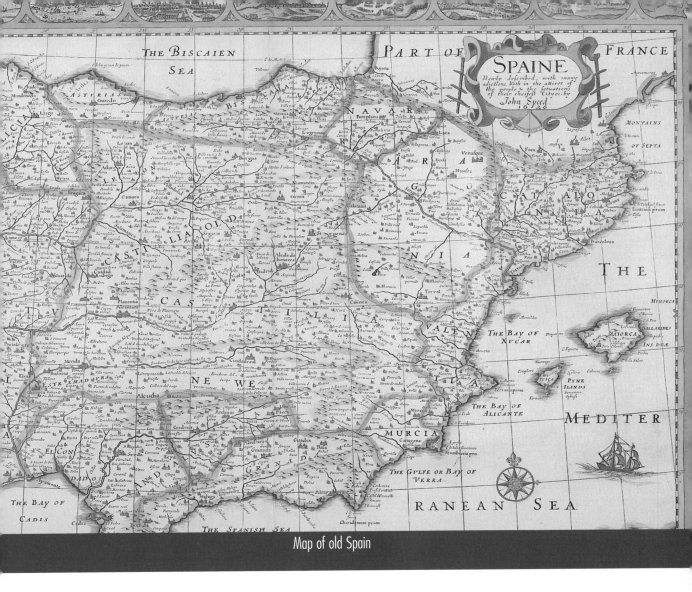

Map of old Spain

Spain became one of the strongest and most important nations in the world.

Much of the wealth Spain gained from the Americas was spent on wars with northern Europe and with the Ottoman Turks in the Mediterranean region. Gradually, the flow of riches from the New World diminished—and so did Spain's power.

CHAPTER TWO—SPAIN'S HISTORY AND GOVERNMENT

Alcázar Castle — also called the Great Ship Castle — where Ferdinand and Isabella once lived

A Decline in Fortunes

During much of the eighteenth and nineteenth centuries, the nations of Europe were at war with one another. At the beginning of this period, when the Bourbon dynasty took the Spanish throne, Spain came under France's influence for nearly a hundred years. Meanwhile, Spain's South American colonies were demanding independence.

In the nineteenth century, when Napoleon Bonaparte's army was defeated during the Peninsular War, Spain regained its independence. The years that followed, however, were filled with unrest. The Spanish people were divided into opposing groups: the country and city people, the **conservatives** and the **liberals**. Violent overthrows of the government happened frequently—but none of the new governments lasted very long.

In the Spanish-American War at the end of the nineteenth century, Spain lost the last of its colonies—Cuba and the Philippines—a loss that proved devastating to Spain's economy and politics. The resulting unrest led to a stronger working class, who, in 1931, forced King Alfonso XIII to **abdicate** his throne. Spain was declared a **republic**—but not everyone was happy about this development. Conservative reaction from both the army and the Catholic Church led to the outbreak of the Spanish civil war. At the end of the

---

Dating Systems and Their Meaning

You might be accustomed to seeing dates expressed with the abbreviations BC or AD, as in the year 1000 BC or the year AD 1900. For centuries, this dating system has been the most common in the Western world. However, since BC and AD are based on Christianity (BC stands for Before Christ and AD stands for *anno Domini*, Latin for "in the year of our Lord"), many people now prefer to use abbreviations that people from all religions can be comfortable using. The abbreviations BCE (meaning Before Common Era) and CE (meaning Common Era), mark time in the same way (for example, 1000 BC is the same year as 1000 BCE, and AD 1900 is the same year as 1900 CE), but BCE and CE do not have the same religious overtones as BC and AD.

---

war, General Francisco Franco and his **nationalist** movement took control of the country.

During World War II, Spain did not openly side with either the Allies or the Axis. Unofficially, however, Franco supported the Axis. As a result, after the war, an international **blockade** was imposed on the country. Spain was **ostracized** from the community of nations, and the Spanish economy sank even lower. Poverty became all too common across the peninsula.

The Return of Good Fortune

During the **Cold War**, Spain became **strategically** attractive to the United States. In the 1950s,

American army bases were built in Spain, and tourists eventually came to Spain along with the military personnel. As foreign money began to flow into Spain, a large middle class emerged, and the nation's desperate poverty diminished.

When Franco died in 1975, the transition to democracy went fairly smoothly. A democratic **constitution** was put in effect in 1978, under the symbolic monarchy of King Juan Carlos II. The young monarch resolutely prodded his nation toward **Western**-style democracy and political reform. Spain's number-one diplomatic goal was to be recognized as a democratic West European society.

When Franco was in power, the European Community had refused to allow Spain to become a member, but now Prime Minister Adolfo Suárez González sent his foreign minister to Brussels to once more ask that Spain be allowed to join. Negotiations for Spain's entry into the European Community were long and complicated. Even after Spain had made many democratic changes to its government, European Community members still worried about how Spain's economy would affect the European Community. Spain's economy was much less developed than that of other member nations, and its industries needed major reforms. Spanish agriculture was also much less developed than it was in the rest of Europe.

After lengthy bargaining, however, these issues were eventually resolved. The Treaty of Accession was signed in the summer of 1985, and on January 1, 1986, Spain finally entered the European Community. The terms of the treaty committed Spain to making major ongoing contributions to the European Community budget, but most Spaniards didn't seem to care. They had finally achieved a long-awaited goal, and now they savored being included in the West European society of nations. As the years went by, polls indicated that most Spaniards had a sense of being "citizens of Europe."

THE PARLIAMENTARY MONARCHY

Today, the Spanish constitution provides for a parliamentary monarchy. The king is a traditional hereditary monarch who acts as head of state and supreme head of the armed forces—but he is not **sovereign**. Instead, sovereign power is held by a two-chamber parliament, called the Cortes, whose members are elected by the citizens.

The Cortes is made up of the Congress of Deputies and the Senate. The Congress of Deputies is the stronger of the two bodies; it consists of three hundred to four hundred members, elected by **proportional representation** every four years (unless the king chooses to call for new elections sooner). The Senate is composed of 208 elected members and 49 regional representatives, who are also elected every four years. Its primary function is territorial representation.

Either house may set a law in motion, but the Congress of Deputies can override a Senate **veto**. This means that if a political party has a solid majority in the Congress of Deputies, they have enormous political clout. The Congress of Deputies also has the power to officially approve or reject legislation, and it acts as a check against the prime minister's power, since the Congress can vote the prime minister out of office. Each chamber of the Cortes meets in separate buildings in Madrid during two regular annual sessions from September to December and from February to June.

The members of the Spanish parliament enjoy certain special privileges: they may not be prosecuted for verbal opinions expressed in the course of their duties; they cannot be arrested for a crime unless they are caught in the actual act of committing it (and even then, the Cortes must give its consent for them to be charged or prosecuted); they are guaranteed a fixed salary and allowances for extra expenses; and they are not obliged to follow their parties' dictates when they cast their votes.

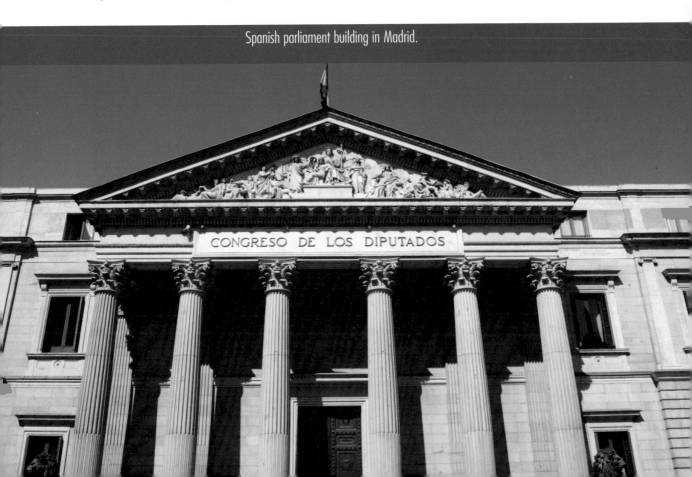

Spanish parliament building in Madrid.

The Congress of Deputies is the lower house of Spanish parliament.

The Royal palace in Madrid.

Meanwhile, the king formally convenes and dissolves the Cortes; he also calls for elections and for **referenda**. He appoints the prime minister after consultation with the Cortes, and he names the other ministers, on the recommendation of the prime minister.

Although the king does not have the power to direct foreign affairs, he has a vital role as the chief representative of Spain in international relations. The potential significance of this role has been demonstrated during the reign of Juan Carlos, whose many trips abroad and contacts with foreign leaders have enabled the Spanish government to establish important political and commercial ties with other nations. The king also has the duty to indicate the state's consent to international treaties and, with the prior authorization of the Cortes, to declare war and peace.

The modern Spanish flag.

While the king has a largely symbolic role, the prime minister is the actual leader of the government. The king has the title of supreme commander of the armed forces, but they are actually under the prime minister's control. Once appointed, the prime minister remains in office until he resigns, loses the support of the Congress of Deputies, or his party is defeated in the general elections.

The prime minister, the deputy prime minister, and the other government ministers make up the Council of Ministers, which is Spain's highest **executive** institution. The Council of Ministers is responsible for putting into effect government policy. It is also responsible for national security and defense. In all its functions, however, it is ultimately responsible to the Cortes. The constitution provides that none of the ministers may engage in professional or commercial activity, or hold any additional public posts. During Franco's reign, senior government officials were often leaders of the business community, which led to corruption.

Today's Spain seeks to avoid the mistakes of the past by maintaining a system of government built carefully on compromise between monarchy and democracy, with a well-structured system of checks and balances.

In the elections of March 1996, the Popular Party (PP) came into power, and José María Aznar became prime minister of the country. He carried out many changes in the government, and during his first term of office, Spain joined the eurozone (the region using the euro as currency). After the terrorist attacks on the United States on September 11, 2001, Aznar allied with the Bush administration in the military actions in Iraq. Under Aznar's leadership, Spain backed the military action against the Taliban in Afghanistan and took a leadership role within the European Union in pushing for increased international cooperation against terrorism.

In 2004, just three days after the terrorist attack on the Madrid commuter train, Aznar's party was voted out of office, and José Luis Rodríguez Zapatero was elected prime minister. Carrying out his campaign promises, Zapatero immediately withdrew Spanish forces from Iraq, but he has continued to support Iraq reconstruction efforts and cooperated with the United States on counterterrorism issues. Zapatero was reelected for a second term as prime minister on March 9, 2008, but he announced in April 2011 that he would not run for reelection in 2012. Mariano Rajoy is Spain's new prime minster.

Puerta de la Duquera, a popular tourist destination

3 THE ECONOMY

During the nineteenth century, when the Industrial Revolution was transforming the economies of most Western European nations,

Spain "missed the boat." Instead, while other nations were turning into modern **mechanized** socities, Spain was deep in social and political turmoil.

At the beginning of the twentieth century, most Spaniards lived in the country, dependent on farming. The country had few factories, and even its farms were not as productive as other West European countries'. Spain lacked technology; its financial institutions were underdeveloped; and the government failed to build the economy. The Spanish civil war wreaked further havoc on the nation's economy, and Franco did very little to help matters once he came into power.

Spain is famous for its citrus fruits.

Not until the 1950s did Spain's economy begin to grow. A second period of economic expansion began in the mid-1980s when Spain entered the European Community (EC, the forerunner of the European Union [EU]). The EC required that Spain modernize its industries, improve its **infrastructure**, and revise its economic laws to conform to EC guidelines. By doing so, Spain was able to reduce its national debt, reduce unemployment from 23 percent to 15 percent in just three years, and reduce **inflation** to less than 3 percent.

In the early twenty-first century, Spain had been transformed from a rural backward nation of farmers into a country with a diverse economy built on manufacturing and service businesses. Beginning in 2007, however, the Spanish economy began to slow down, then taking massive damage in the financial crisis of 2008 and 2009. The economy of Spain is now the fifth largest in Europe, accounting for about 9 percent of the EU's total financial output. Spain's **per capita** income is just below the EU average.

QUICK FACTS: THE ECONOMY OF SPAIN

Gross Domestic Product (GDP): US$1.411 trillion (2011 est.)

GDP per capita: US$30,600 (2011 est.)

Industries: textiles and apparel (including footwear), food and beverages, metals and metal manufactures, chemicals, shipbuilding, automobiles, machine tools, tourism, clay and refractory products, footwear, pharmaceuticals, medical equipment

Agriculture: grain, vegetables, olives, wine grapes, sugar beets, citrus; beef, pork, poultry, dairy products; fish

Export commodities: machinery, motor vehicles; foodstuffs, pharmaceuticals, medicines, other consumer goods

Export partners: France 18.7%, Germany 10.7%, Portugal 9.1%, Italy 9%, UK 6.3% (2010)

Import commodities: machinery and equipment, fuels, chemicals, semifinished goods; foodstuffs, consumer goods, measuring and medical control instruments

Import partners: Germany 12.6%, France 11.5%, Italy 7.3%, China 6.8%, Netherlands 5.6%, UK 4.9% (2010)

Currency: euro (EUR)

Currency exchange rate: US$1 = 0.7107 EUR (2011)

Note: All figures are from 2011 unless otherwise noted.
Source: www.cia.gov, 2012.

EXPORTS AND IMPORTS

Spain's most important trading partners are France, Germany, and Italy. Its chief exports are machinery, including motor vehicles, and food products. The country is the world's largest producer of olive oil, the fourth largest of dried fruit, and the sixth largest of citrus fruits. Spain's vineyards are the largest in the world, although it's only the fifth-highest producer of wine-grapes and ranks third in wine production. Its other important crops include barley, wheat, maize, rice, potatoes, sugar beets, peppers, avocados, tomatoes, tobacco, hops, oil-bearing fruits, and cork. Meanwhile, Spain imports machinery and equipment, fuels, chemicals, food, and consumer goods.

INDUSTRIES

Just five of Spain's provinces (Barcelona, Biscay, Madrid, Navarre, and Oviedo, all located in the north and east) produce over half the country's manufacturing output. The Catalonia region, where some 85 percent of companies are located in Barcelona, is Spain's economic powerhouse and one of Europe's most important industrial regions.

Spanish industry is rooted in small and medium-sized family businesses; just a few Spanish businesses are known internationally (Telefónica, Endesa, Repsol, and others). Most Spanish manufacturers are too small to compete globally. As a result, Spain has relied heavily on foreign investment (three-quarters of it in Barcelona and Madrid) for much of its recent growth.

The Spanish economy is hindered by its lack of modern machinery and technology; many Spanish industrial plants are out of date, with machinery that needs replacing. Spain has had particular difficulty developing computer technology, which puts the nation's industries at a definite disadvantage. Poor efficiency and lack of good business organization further weaken Spanish industries.

Spain's most important industries include tourism, chemicals and petrochemicals, **heavy industry**, and food and beverages. Its principal growth areas include tourism, insurance, and electronics. Tourism is one of Spain's most important industries, especially in Andalusia.

Once the richest nation in Europe, over the past few centuries Spain has endured poverty and economic recessions. Spain's economy paid the cost for the country's isolation from the rest of the world through much of the nineteenth and twentieth centuries.

Then, with the coming of democracy, the Spanish economy was regarded as one of the strongest within the EU. However, the economy depended on its tourism industry, housing market, and construction industry; the global economic crisis of 2008 through 2009 hit the country hard, because fewer people could afford to travel and buy and build new homes.

Spain's economy plunged into recession, and by mid-2010, unemployment there was double the EU average. Spaniards were angry about the **austerity** measures imposed by their government to reduce the nation's debt. The future looked bleak unless Spain's people could find a way through their problems.

Tourists flock to Spain's many beaches.

A bullring in Ronda, Spain

4 SPAIN'S PEOPLE AND CULTURE

For centuries, Spain's people lacked any true uni-
fied identity. Its regions with their varied climates
and   geography   joined   in   a   loose
federation, but not until modern times .did .
Spaniards begin to identify themselves with their
nation rather than their particular region. Even
today, Spain's regions have their own cultural, economic, and political characteristics—and people

still feel that their primary loyalty lies with their town or region, and only secondarily with Spain as a whole.

SPAIN'S POPULATION GROUPS

Around the edges of the Iberian Peninsula are groups of people who have competed for centuries for control of the peninsula. The Portuguese to the west are the only group that successfully established its own state (in 1640). The Galicians live along the northwest, and the Asturians are on the northern coast of the Bay of Biscay. The Basques live near the coast toward France; the Navarrese and the Aragonese are along the Pyrenees backbone; the Catalans are in the north-

Spanish women in traditional costumes

east; the Valencians in the east; and in the south are the Andalusians.

Rich Spain and Poor Spain

Economic differences divide Spaniards even more than the cultural differences between the various regions. For the past century, the government has tried to redistribute the country's wealth more fairly, but these differences continue to exist.

If you drew an imaginary line from the middle of the north coast southeast to Madrid and then to Valencia, you could mark the invisible boundary that has existed between "Rich Spain" and "Poor Spain." To the north and east of the line lived the wealthy Spaniards in an area that was modern, industrial, and urban. By the 1980s, this region was already transitioning to a thriving information and services economy. But to the south and west of that imaginary line lies "Poor Spain," where most people supported themselves by farming. Social conditions here were much different from what they were on the rich side. The separation between the two groups grew even wider when the people of Rich Spain tended to think of themselves as culturally "not-Spanish."

Religion

Despite their differences, Spaniards have one big thing in common: almost all of them (about 94 percent) are Roman Catholic. Back in the fifteenth century, when Ferdinand and Isabella conquered Muslim Spain, they established Catholicism as the national religion. During the **Inquisition**, Jews and Muslims who refused to convert were expelled from Spain. Even those Muslims who did convert (called Moriscos) were expelled in the early 1600s. This left only the Catholics.

Today, however, few Spanish Catholics take their religion quite as seriously as Ferdinand and Isabella did. Catholic ceremonies and festivals are still vital to the flavor of Spanish culture. Though most people get married in the church, and they baptize their children, few Spaniards attend church regularly these days. They look to Catholic traditions to give their lives depth and meaning, but they tend to not seek practical direction from the Church's teachings.

Spanish Arts and Culture

Architecture

Spain is famous for its architecture, particularly its Gothic churches and medieval castles. Even the smallest towns have their own distinctive architectural atmosphere. Every town and village has a plaza mayor—main square—often reached by an **arcade**. The square is usually an extended open courtyard of the town or village hall. From prehis-

Quick Facts: The People of Spain

Population: 47,042,984 (July 2012 est.)
Ethnic groups: composite of Mediterranean and Nordic types
Age structure:
   0–14 years: 15.1%
   15–64 years: 67.7%
   65 years and over: 17.1% (2011 est.)
Population growth rate: 0.654% (2012 est.)
Birth rate: 10.4 births/1,000 population (2012 est.)
Death rate: 8.88 deaths/1,000 population (July 2012 est.)
Migration rate: 5.02 migrant(s)/1,000 population (2012 est.)
Infant mortality rate: 3.37 deaths/1,000 live births
Life expectancy at birth:
   Total population: 81.27 years
   Male: 78.26 years
   Female: 84.47 years (2012 est.)
Total fertility rate: 1.48 children born/woman (2012 est.)
Religions: Roman Catholic 94%, other 6%
Languages: Castilian Spanish 74% (official language nationwide), Catalan 17%, Galician 7%, Basque 2%
Literacy rate: 97.9% (2003)

Note: All figures are from 2011 unless otherwise noted.
Source: www.cia.gov, 2012.

Velázquez (1599–1660) and Goya (1746–1828), who played a significant role in the evolution of painting in Europe. Works by these artists and many others can be seen at the Prado art museum in Madrid. In the twentieth century, Spain's Paris School produced such internationally known names as Salvador Dalí and Pablo Picasso.

The country is also famous for its talented craftsmen. They create carved furniture (particularly chests); tapestries and embroideries; gold, silver, and ironwork (including wrought-iron screens); sculpture; and ceramics.

Music

Spain has a rich musical heritage. The guitar was invented in Andalusia in the 1790s when a sixth string was added to the Moorish lute. By the 1870s, the guitar had gained its modern shape. Spanish musicians have taken the guitar to heights of virtuosity and none more so than Andrés Segovia (1893–1997), who established classical guitar as a musical genre.

Guitars are essential to flamenco, Spain's best-known musical tradition. Flamenco has its roots in the *cante jondo* (deep song) of the Roma of

toric monuments in the Balearic Islands to Roman ruins to fantastic modernist constructions, Spain's architecture is some of the most impressive in the world.

Visual Arts

Ever since the tenth century, Spain has produced great painters. Two of the most famous are

The Sagrada Família basilica in Barcelona is a good example of Spain's more modern architecture.

One of Pablo Picasso's most famous works is *Guernica* (1937), a massive painting commissioned by the Spanish government that depicts the bombing of the Basque city of Guernica. Picasso's canvas is a vivid and brutal portrayal of people, animals, and buildings wrenched by the violent bombing. The painting has become a larger symbol for the entire world, for it embodies the inhumanity and hopelessness of war.

Modern composers such as Enrique Granados, Isaac Albéniz, Manuel de Falla, and Joaquín Rodrigo have also gained international recognition. Plácido Domingo is one of Spain's most famous operatic performers, closely followed by José Carreras. Cataluña's Montserrat Caballé is known to be one of the most outstanding sopranos in the world.

LITERATURE

Spain's most famous author is Miguel Cervantes, who wrote *Don Quixote de la Mancha*. This seventeenth-century book is one of the earliest novels written in a modern European language, and many people consider it still to be the finest work ever written in the Spanish language.

The book tells the story of Don Quixote and his squire, Sancho Panza. Don Quixote is obsessed with stories of knights, and his friends and family think he's crazy when he sets out to wander across Spain on Rocinante, his skinny Andalusia, but today it is experiencing a revival. Paco de Lucía is an internationally known flamenco guitarist, and Pablo Casals is an equally gifted cellist.

horse, righting wrongs and protecting the oppressed.

Don Quixote sees reality with the eyes of a romantic. He believes ordinary inns are enchanted castles, and peasant girls are beautiful princesses. His head-in-the-clouds dreaminess has become a part of the entire world's imagination. Even in the English language, the word "quixotic," from Don Quixote's name, means "idealistic and impractical." The expression "tilting at windmills" also comes from this story.

SPANISH PASTIMES

People in Spain love to go to the movies. They also enjoy plays, and most cities have theatres. Many of these were built by the socialist government in the 1980s and '90s.

One of the most important sports in Spain is football—or soccer, as it's called in North America. Around 300,000 spectators attend the games in the Primera División, and millions more follow the games on television. People gamble on the football results through the quiniela or football pools.

La corrida de toros—the bullfight—may be considered cruel in North American culture, but it still has a tremendous following in Spain. It gained enormous popularity in the mid-eighteenth century, when breeders developed the first breeds of *toro bravo* or fighting bulls, and it still plays a vital role in Spanish culture.

SPANISH EATING HABITS

Spaniards usually start the day with a very light breakfast (*desayuno*), often little more than coffee;

they have brunch (*almuerzo*) around 10:30 A.M.; lunch (*comida*) between 1:30 P.M. and 4 P.M.; and dinner (*cena*) is as late as 10 or 11 P.M. Cafés are the centers of social activity in most cities and villages.

Tapas are also an important part of the Spaniards' way of life. These are little snacks that include things such as *calamares* (squid), *callos* (tripe), *gambas* (prawns), *albóndigas* (meatballs), and *boquerones* (anchovies) marinated in vinegar. Tapas can be taken as a meal in themselves or as a tasty bite before dinner. Each region of Spain has its own tapa specialties. Tapas bars have become popular eating places in the United States.

For centuries, Spain has been one of the world's great cultural centers. Its ancient roots in Africa and Rome, as well as Europe, have given it a unique flavor all its own. Because of its many colonies in the Americas, today Spain's influence still reaches around the globe.

What Does "Tapa" Mean?

The actual translation of tapa is "lid." The story goes that bar owners used to cover drinks with a piece of bread to keep the flies away. It then became practice to put a tidbit of meat on the bread—and this evolved into the tapas of today.

The bullfight plays a major role in Spanish culture.

The Mediterranean Sea plays a vital role in Barcelona's commerce.

5 CHAPTER SPAIN'S FUTURE

Antonio Moreno is a Spaniard. And he's a Roma, a Gypsy.

Antonio knows that if he lived in France or many of the other nations in the EU he would face discrimination and prejudice—but less so in Spain. Spain, with all of its many problems, has found positive ways to address the Roma's problems. "I'm first Spanish, then Gypsy," Antonio told Time magazine, "and I'm proud to be both . . . it's better here than anywhere else I've seen. Spain has helped Gypsies a lot."

WHO ARE THE ROMA?

About a thousand years ago, groups of people migrated from northern India, spreading across Europe over the next several centuries. Though these people actually came from several different tribes (the largest of which were the Sinti and Roma), the people of Europe called them simply "Gypsies"—a shortened version of "Egyptians," since people thought they came from Egypt.

Europeans were frightened of these dark-skinned, non-Christian people who spoke a foreign language. Unlike the settled people of Europe, the Roma were wanderers, with no ties to the land. Europeans did not understand them. Stories and stereotypes grew up about the Gypsies, and these fanned the flames of prejudice and discrimination. Many of these same stories and stereotypes are still believed today.

Throughout the centuries, non-Gypsies continually tried to either assimilate the Gypsies or kill them. Attempts to assimilate the Gypsies involved stealing their children and placing them with other families; giving them cattle and feed, expecting them to become farmers; outlawing their customs, language, and clothing, and forcing them to attend school and church. In many ways the Roma of Europe were treated much as the European settlers treated the Native peoples of North America.

Many European laws allowed—or even commanded—the killing of Gypsies. A practice of "Gypsy hunting"—similar to fox hunting—was both common and legal in some parts of Europe. Even as late as 1835, a Gypsy hunt in Denmark "brought in a bag of over 260 men, women, and children." But the worst of all crimes against the Roma happened in the twentieth century, when Hitler's Third Reich sent them to concentration camps. As many as half a million Gypsies died in the Nazis' death camps.

THE ROMA IN SPAIN

Things weren't always like this for the Roma in Spain, though. During Franco's dictatorship, the Roma weren't allowed to work, go to school, or even gather in groups larger than four people. "We weren't even human," Antonio says. "We were animals." But today the EU and the Roma themselves all agree that Spain has become a model for integrating Gypsies into its society. Other countries in the EU—Bulgaria, Slovakia, Hungary, the Czech Republic, and Romania—are looking to Spain for ideas to help them build a better future for the Roma who live in their nations.

Of the 10 to 12 million Roma who live in Europe, Spain has almost a million (about 2 percent of its total population). The country spends almost €36 million (about $48 million) each year providing services to support the Roma. In Spain, only 5 percent of Roma live in makeshift camps and substandard housing the way they do in many European nations; most Spanish Roma have access to health care; and at least 75 percent have jobs.

Spain believes that the Roma are an important part of its future. That's why the government invests in education for Roma children, which is one of the key factors in keeping Roma adults out of poverty. The Roma can have access to public housing and financial aid on the condition that they send their children to schools and health-care facilities—and as a result, almost all Spanish Gypsy children go to school, and 85 percent of adult Spanish Roma can read and write. Another Spanish program works with young, unemployed Gypsies, teaching them technical skills, helping them earn the equivalent of a high school degree, and finally placing them in jobs with private companies. However, that doesn't mean that Spanish Roma don't ever encounter prejudice from other Spaniards.

Many Roma throughout Europe move from country to country, but Spain's Roma population tends to stay put because Spain is doing a good job at meeting their needs. Antonio Moreno, along with many other Roma, is committed to Spain's future. "We're staying in Spain," he says, ". . . this is our home."

The Economy

The most immediate problem facing Spain as a nation is its economic issues. Spain was the last major economy to move out of a recession, and by 2012, it was back in recession. Spain's government announced in 2012 that it planned to put into effect billions of euros of spending cuts, hoping to reduce the country's deficit to 5.3 percent of gross domestic product (GDP) from 8.5 percent in 2011. The prime minister warned the Spanish people that they were facing a "very, very austere budget." In response to these announcements from their government, strikers took to the streets of several Spanish cities across the country. Earlier in 2012, the government had passed other labor laws that gave more rights to employers while taking them away from workers. Spain's people were worried. As it moves into the future, Spain must figure out how to balance government spending with providing the services that its citizens expect. Economists, the EU, and Spaniards themselves are all keeping an eye on Spain's economic future.

Climate Change

One of the big problems that threatens the future of the entire planet is global climate change. Spain has many strengths and it is working hard to overcome its problems—but the future for us all depends on the Earth's well-being. We can't fix the economy or society if we don't have a place to live!

Climate change could have enormous negative effects on Spain and its economy. Some scientists estimate that over the next twenty to thirty-five years, the rising sea levels caused by climate change could destroy about half of Spain's beaches; heat waves, floods, tornados, droughts, and other extreme weather will increase; and all this will make the country a much less attractive spot for tourists. Without its tourist industry, Spain's economy will be in trou-

What Is Global Climate Change—and Why Are People So Worried About It?

Global climate change has to do with an average increase in the Earth's temperature. Most scientists agree that humans are responsible because of the pollution cars and factories have put into the air.

Global warming is already having serious impacts on humans and the environment in many ways. An increase in global temperatures causes rising sea levels (because of melting of the polar caps) and changes in the amount and pattern of precipitation. These changes may increase the frequency and intensity of extreme weather events, such as floods, droughts, heat waves, hurricanes, and tornados. Other consequences include changes to farms' crop production, species becoming extinct, and an increased spread of disease.

Not all experts agree about climate change, but almost all scientists believe that it is very real. Politicians and the public do not agree, though, on policies to deal with climate change. Changes in the way people live can be expensive, at both the personal and national levels, and not everyone is convinced that taking on these expenses needs to be a priority.

ble. Farming will also suffer as a result of climate change.

Spain's government recognizes that climate change will cause water shortages. With help from the EU, Spain is building desalination plants to try to deal with this problem. Not all experts agree, however, that this is a good idea. **Ecologists** warn that **desalination** uses up a lot of energy, and it also puts carbon dioxide into the atmosphere (which will further contribute to global warming). Many experts recommend that Spain instead build the technology for capturing and storing its rainwater.

The EU has **sustainable energy** goals for all its member nations. Spain will have a hard time complying with these goals. Farmers and industries tend to want short-term solutions, rather than paying the price for long-term answers.

But Spain remains committed to the European Union. It knows that by saying yes to the EU, Spain is also saying yes to the future.

Desalination stations like this one convert salt water to fresh water by removing salt and other minerals.

Time Line

8000–4000 BCE	Iberians move into Spain.
800 BCE	Celts arrive at the northern part of the Iberian Peninsula.
206 BCE	Roman Empire invades Spain.
4th century CE	Spain becomes Christian.
711–1248	Moors occupy the Iberian Peninsula.
854 CE	Madrid is established.
1085	Madrid's Muslim era ends.
1474	Marriage of Queen Isabella and King Ferdinand unite Castilian and Aragonese realms to create the original nation of Spain.
1492	Granada falls to Queen Isabella and King Ferdinand. Queen Isabella and King Ferdinand finance Christopher Columbus's trip to the New World.
1561	Madrid becomes permanent seat of the royal court.
1605	Part 1 of Miguel de Cervantes' novel *Don Quixote* is made available to the public. Part 2 was released in 1615.
1713	Spain cedes Gibraltar to Great Britain.
1790s	The guitar is invented in Andalusia.
1888	World's Fair is held in Barcelona.
1929	Seville hosts the Latin American Exhibition.

1931	King Alfonso XIII abdicates the Spanish throne and Spain is declared a republic.
1942	Ferdinand Franco assumes complete control of Spain.
1951	The Treaty of Paris is signed, forming the core of what would become the EU.
1957	The Treaties of Rome forms the European Economic Community.
1958	Spain joins the Organisation for European Economic Co-operation.
1959	Basque Fatherland and Liberty (ETA) forms. Spain joins the World Bank.
1975	Ferdinand Franco dies and is succeeded by King Juan Carlos II.
1978	Spain's constitution creates the Cortes.
1986	Spain joins the European Community.
1992	The European Union is formed under the Maastricht Treaty.
1995 and 2002	Spain's president serves as president of the European Union.
March 2004	Terrorist bomb on the Madrid train system kills almost two hundred people.
2005	Spain is the first country to vote in favor of a new European charter.
2006	The ETA is responsible for a deadly bombing to Madrid's international airport.
2008	Global recession spreads around the world.
2011	The ETA commits to a permanent ceasefire.
	Spain's parliament votes to prohibit the burqa in all public places.
	Spanish youth in 150 cities protest unemployment and social welfare cutbacks.

FIND OUT MORE

IN BOOKS

Cervantes, Miguel de. *Don Quixote*. New York: Barnes and Noble Books, 2004.
Davis, Kevin A. *Look What Came from Spain*. New York: Watts Franklin, 2003.
Rogers, Lura. *Spain*. New York: Scholastic Library Publishing, 2001.
Williams, Mark R. *Story of Spain*. Chandler, Ariz.: Golden Era Books, 2004.

ON THE INTERNET

Travel Information
www.lonelyplanet.com/destinations/Europe/spain/

History and Geography
www.red2000.com/spain/primer/hist.html
www.countryreports.org/history/spaihist.htm

Economic and Political Information
countrystudies.us/spain/81.htm

Culture and Festivals
www.donquijote.org/culture/spain
www.spain-info.com/Culture

Publisher's note:
The websites listed on this page were active at the time of publication. The publisher is not responsible for websites that have changed their addresses or discontinued operation since the date of publication. The publisher will review and update the website list upon each reprint.

GLOSSARY

abdicate: Resign a position.

acquitted: Freed from criminal charges.

activists: People who are willing to take action to bring about positive change.

apprenticeships: Legal agreements to work for another for a specific amount of time in return for instruction in a trade, art, or business.

arcade: A covered passageway with arches along the side.

austerity: A government a policy of deficit-cutting, lower spending, and a reduction in the amount of benefits and public services provided.

barbarian: A member of a people whose culture and behavior were considered uncivilized.

blockade: An organized action to prevent people or goods from entering or leaving a place.

Cold War: The hostile, nonviolent relationship between the former Soviet Union and the United States, and their respective allies, between 1946 and 1989.

conquistadors: Spanish conquerors of the Americas.

conservative: Unwilling to accept abrupt change, preferring instead to maintain things the way they are.

constitution: A country's written statement outlining the basic laws and principles by which it is governed.

corruption: Dishonest conduct by those in power, typically involving bribery.

desalination: The process of removing salt from ocean water.

defendants: The individuals on trial.

democratic: Having to do with a system of government by the people, usually through elected representatives.

discrimination: Unfair treatment of a person or group, especially because of prejudice about race, ethnicity, age, or gender.

ecologists: A scientist who studies the relationship between plants and animals and their environment.

economic: Having to do with all the wealth and resources of a nation or region.

executive: The section of a country's government responsible for implementing decisions relating to laws.

extremists: People willing to take extreme measures to bring about change.

galleys: Large ships used for war or trading in the Mediterranean Sea during the Middle Ages.

heavy industry: The manufacture of large heavy objects and materials in bulk.

human rights: The freedoms to which all people are entitled.

industrialized: Having factories on a large scale basis.

inflation: An economic condition in which the supply of money or credit is greater the amount of goods and services available for purchase, causing things to cost more.

infrastructure: A country's large-scale public systems, services, and facilities that are necessary for economic growth and development.

Inquisition: A thirteenth-century organization in the Roman Catholic Church formed to find, question, and sentence those who did not hold mainstream religious beliefs.

liberals: People who are tolerant of different views and standards, and who favor political reforms that extend democracy, distribute wealth more evenly, and protect personal freedoms.

mechanized: Equipped with machines.

nationalist: Having to do with extreme patriotism.

Neanderthal: A member of an extinct subspecies of humans that lived in Europe, northern Africa, and western Asia in the early Stone Age.

negotiate: Try to reach an agreement through discussion.

ostracized: Banished or excluded from society or from a particular group.

parliament: A national government that represents the people, which has supreme authority to make a country's laws.

per capita: For each person.

prejudice: Unfair opinions based on race, gender, or religion.

proportional representation: An electoral system in which each party's share of seats in government is the same as its share of all the votes cast.

radical: Extreme, going against what is considered socially normal.

recession: A period of economic slowdown when businesses stop growing or go out of business, causing an increase in unemployment.

referenda: Votes by the whole of an electorate on a specific question or questions put to it by a government.

republic: A form of government in which people elect representatives to exercise power for them.

separatist: In favor of breaking or staying away from a country or group.

socialist: Having to do with a political and economic theory that advocates that the means of production, distribution, and exchange should be owned or regulated by the community as a whole (the government) rather than by individuals.

sovereign: Self-governing and independent.

strategically: Having to do with a long-term plan or goal.

sustainable energy: Conserving a balance within nature by avoiding the depletion of natural resources; able to be continued indefinitely.

terrorism: The use of violence and fear to bring about political goals.

veto: The power of one branch of government to reject the legislation of another.

Western: Relating to countries, primarily in Europe and North and South America, whose culture and society are greatly influenced by traditions rooted in Greek and Roman culture and in Christianity.

INDEX

Picture Credits

ABOUT THE AUTHORS

Rae Simons has written several nonfiction children's books, as well as children's and adult fiction. She speaks Spanish and enjoys learning about other countries and cultures.

Shaina Carmel Indovino is a writer and illustrator living in Nesconset, New York. She graduated from Binghamton University, where she received degrees in sociology and English. Shaina has enjoyed the opportunity to apply both of her fields of study to her writing, and she hopes readers will benefit from taking a look at the countries of the world through more than one perspective.

About the Series Consultant

Ambassador John Bruton served as Irish Prime Minister from 1994 until 1997. As prime minister, he helped turn Ireland's economy into one of the fastest-growing in the world. He was also involved in the Northern Ireland Peace Process, which led to the 1998 Good Friday Agreement. During his tenure as Ireland's prime minister, he also presided over the European Union presidency in 1996 and helped finalize the Stability and Growth Pact, which governs management of the euro. Before being named the European Commission Head of Delegation in the United States, he was a member of the convention that drafted the European Constitution, signed October 29, 2004.

The European Commission Delegation to the United States represents the interests of the European Union as a whole, much as ambassadors represent their countries' interests to the U.S. government. Matters coming under European Commission authority are negotiated between the commission and the U.S. administration.